—1932—
FORD STREET RODS

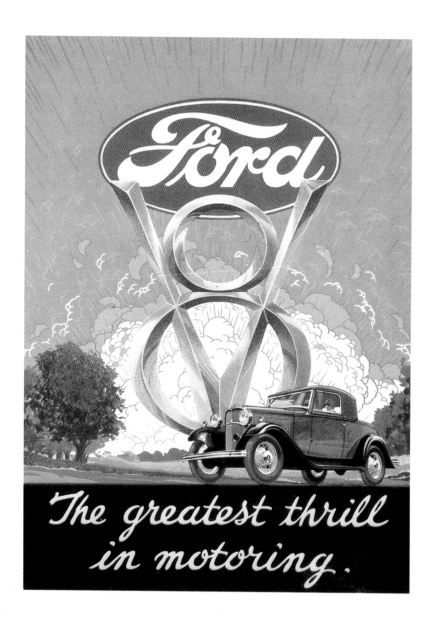

The greatest thrill in motoring.

Osprey Colour Series

-1932-
FORD STREET RODS

Mike Key

Published in 1986 by Osprey Publishing Limited
27A Floral Street, London WC2E 9DP
Member company of the George Philip Group

British Library Cataloguing in Publication Data

Key, Mike
    Ford Street Rods, 1932
    1. Ford automobile—History
    I. Title
    629.2'222   TL215.F7
ISBN 0-85045-732-7

Editor Tony Thacker
Design David Tarbutt

Printed in Hong Kong

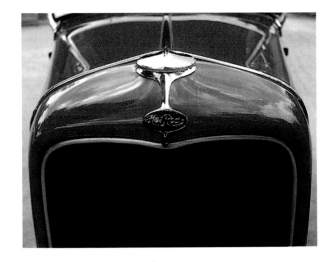

FRONT COVER *This beautiful candy-wine Cabriolet is
the proud possession of Jim Talaga of Illinois, and is
somewhat unusual in that it has coil-sprung rear
suspension and 302 cubic inches of Ford power*

PAGE 1 *British Ford advertising poster from 1932*
PREVIOUS PAGE *The owner of this blown hi-boy gets on
the gas*
ABOVE *Modified badge says it all*
BACK COVER *Another hi-boy on the highway*

About the author

Mike started his career at Santa Pod Raceway in England photographing the drag races. Through that sport he was introduced to street rods and decided that he just had to have one. His first attempt was a T-bucket appropriately named *Fotofantasy* but whilst it was a neat car Mike knew it wasn't exactly the right stuff. The right stuff was a '32 Ford and Mike found his, an English Tudor, in a barn in Beccles, not far from his home in Heathersett, Norfolk.

Mike's B became one of England's first rodded Deuces when he dropped the front end, suspended the rear on a Jaguar IRS and junked the four in favour of a 327 cu. in. Chevy. The car has been on the road for more than ten years now but it is about to undergo a complete rebuild, perhaps with a new set of Deuce Factory rails. Though they might go under a rotted-out Fordor he found which would make the ideal base for a Phaeton. Something we never had in England.

In the intervening years he's managed to rod a '40 Chevy sedan for himself, several VWs for his

ABOVE *With suicide doors Mike's Tudor is instantly recognizable as English. He pulled it from an old barn in Norfolk, England, replaced the original four with a 327 cu. in. Chevy, the I-beam with a four-inch dropped SuperBell, and the rear end with that from an S-type Jaguar. The car has seen more than ten years' regular service but Mike is now in the process of rebuilding it*

wife June and develop his freelance photography to such an extent that he now supplies features to many of the world's rodding magazines.

I've known Mike for almost ten years now and I'm happy to say we've been good friends and confidents, especially when times have been difficult, as they so often are in this business. Sometimes magazines fold before you can blink, certainly before any cheque arrives. Nevertheless, Mike keeps bouncing back and it is that energy which makes him such a likeable character. But what I want to know is, when is he going to do something about that '40 Plymouth coupé he has stashed away at the bottom of the garden?

Tony Thacker

When Henry Ford invented his T model he not only introduced us to mass production but he brought transport to the masses. He also gave the masses, at least those who wanted it, the means to go motor racing on the cheap.

Prior to this motor racing had been the privilege of the rich but suddenly it became the prerogative of the poorer classes. Henry wasn't that keen on racing but he liked to build and sell cars with plenty of acceleration and that was what the public liked. In fact they wanted more speed than was available so pretty soon a speed equipment industry, producing high performance camshafts, cylinder heads and carburettors, was established, albeit working mainly from backyard engineering shops.

By the late 1920s Lizzie, as the T was affectionately known, was an old woman and, though reluctant, Henry replaced her with a new lady, the Model A. The A was an altogether different car from its predecessor, it had style and it had a new four-cylinder engine which was twice

as powerful as the T. As good as it was it was not the sensation the T had been. Henry, therefore, secretly began development of a new low-priced V8 which could be mass produced. It would be another engineering first for Ford.

Initially the plan was to merely drop the V8 into an improved A model, Henry not being particularly interested in body design and styling. His son Edsel, however, excelled in this area and with the aid of designer Eugene Gregorie developed a pleasing design reminiscent of Ford's big brother Lincoln.

When introduced in March the 1932 Ford Models B (four-cylinder) and 18 (V8) caused a sensation, Ford claiming 5½ million viewers attended nationwide showings. Unfortunately the world was still in the grips of the Great Depression and though the public might have wished to avail themselves of Ford's new 65 hp hot rod, most of them could not afford to.

The general public might not have been able to afford the new models but somehow racers always

seem able to find the money and pretty soon after its introduction B, and to some extent V8, engines began to appear on American racetracks.

At the time, American auto racing was restricted almost exclusively to oval tracks. In most cases these were mile or half-mile dirt tracks used for horse racing but in some cases they were banked wooden-board ovals built for cycle or motorcycle racing. The pinnacle of American oval track racing was the Indianapolis 500, held annually on a brick-built autodrome.

Whilst the T, and to some extent the A, did well in the dirt, Fords had never fared well at the brickyard. Several cars raced there in the early 1930s in the 'stock block' formula but none even finished.

Then in August 1933 the American Automobile Association reinstated, for the first time since 1920, the Elgin Road Race for Stock Cars. Though one could hardly call them stock, stripped of their windshields and mudguards/fenders, they were to all intents and purposes production cars.

Ford had, earlier that year, introduced the Model 40, a development of the 1932 models. Besides a

ABOVE *The dust and the glory. This is where it all began on the dry lake beds of the Mojave Desert in Southern California. This pre-war photograph is typical of the times when hundreds of rodders would ride out to the desert to race their hot rods. Almost all were roadsters though specially built racers were beginning to appear in the late 1930s. The SCTA still sanction races at the lakes. Photograph courtesy of Frank Oddo*

OPPOSITE PAGE *The fine, white alkali dust kicked up by the cars was not washed off, being an indication to those in town that this was a lakes racer. This picture shows Veda Orr in 1941. Veda's husband Karl was the first to exceed 120 mph and the car eventually ran 125.82 mph. Photograph courtesy of Frank Oddo*

new body which precedented annual body changes, the 40 had an improved V8 which now produced 85 hp in standard form. Supposedly the engine in Elgin-winner Fred Frame's '33 Roadster was a special supplied out of Ford's back door. Only eight of the 15 starters finished but the first seven cars home were Fords and several of those were '32 models. The action moved then to Los Angeles, California, where at Mines Field Ford took the first ten places. A month later another Ford, in the hands of Lou Meyer, won the American Targa Florio which sadly was to be the last road race in the US for many years.

Nevertheless, the V8 was now established as an engine with racing potential, it having been almost ignored by another group of racers because they already had more powerful T and A engines with aftermarket ohv conversions. Compared to Indy racers these guys were the poorest of the poor because in the main they were racing their daily drivers. Their venue was the dry lakes of California's Mojave Desert.

Every weekend they would drive their stripped-down, hopped-up Roadsters the 100 or so miles over the San Gabriel mountains into the desert. There in the early morning, before the sun grew too hot, they would time their cars for classification. Then everybody would line up and race across the lake bed. Unfortunately only those out in front could see, those behind were shrouded in fine alkali dust. Understandably the ensuing mêlée was incredibly dangerous and many a young racer lost his life.

Born out of this amateur enthusiasm, however, was another Ford-inspired speed equipment industry which would, over the ensuing years, develop into a major American industry. Many of the men who produced the cams, heads and carbs

BELOW *Karl also owned this speed shop which supplied those all-important cams, heads and carbs initially to the racers but eventually to guys who just wanted to cruise.* Photograph courtesy of Frank Oddo

RIGHT *The turning point for street rodding was the introduction of organized drag racing. This picture shows two Roadsters lined up at the Blimp Base in El Toro in 1950.* Photograph courtesy of Pat Ganahl

of the time became household names in the hot rod hall of fame.

The accidents were a problem though, as was the enthusiasm for speed on the street both going to, returning from and between lakes meets. The racers didn't even bother to wash the dust from their cars, preferring to keep it as a proud boast of their racing exploits. If they didn't clean their cars they certainly weren't going to bother rebuilding them, so they ran around the streets with tuned engines, loud exhausts and minimal bodywork. There were even those who couldn't be bothered to drive out to the lakes to race so their activities, coupled with the accidents and the general illegality of the cars, soon attracted the attention of the police.

Before they could be banned the rodders organized themselves and late in 1937 formed the Southern California Timing Association. They had a newspaper, a few rules and they organized the lakes racing until the outbreak of war.

In Europe and the rest of the world the 1932 Ford performed equally well, its excellent power-to-weight ratio standing it in good stead for every type of motoring event from hillclimbs to the Monte Carlo Rally. Unfortunately the Depression was, if anything, worse in Europe than America and even had the public been able to afford them, European governments discouraged imports of American cars. Though there was a faithful following, the Ford V8 never enjoyed the popularity in the rest of the world that it received in the US.

Continued on page 15

LEFT *Who said there's nothing new about nostalgia? Steve Centracchio, a member of the 'Flyin' Flatheads' from West Springfield, Massachusetts, has only recently pulled the Olds engine from his purple people-pleaser Cabriolet in favour of this new old-timey engine. Twenty-four studder sports Edelbrock heads, S.C.O.T. blower, twin Stromberg 97s and Scintilla mag. Other 1950s touches include three-inch top chop, shaved handles, filled shell and King Bee headlights*

ABOVE *Two of a kind. These two identical hi-boy Roadsters are owned by National Street Rod Association executives Vernon Walker and Gilbert Bugg, both of Memphis, Tennessee. Both cars are powered by Buick V6 engines and both are suspended on buggy springs at the front and triangulated four-link systems with coil-overs at the rear*

11

LEFT *Cruising Columbus, Ohio—Tudor style. With three-piece hood, dropped headlight bar, Moon discs reflecting the sunlight and that triple-ripple bumper pushing gravel*

BOTTOM LEFT *Clockwork Orange is a very English assembly using a fibreglass body and the chassis and I-beam front axle from a 1935 Austin, a Jaguar 420G independent rear end, but all-American power in the form of a 390 cu. in. Ford V8. Interestingly the front shocks are tiny units mounted vertically just inside the grille. In the hands of owner Martin Holden it has run a best time of 11.99 on the strip using a squirt of laughing gas*

BELOW *British boy Ian Gibson built this fibreglass-bodied Roadster in eight months. It uses Deuce Factory rails, Mark 2 Jaguar live rear axle, American Street Rod Parts buggy-sprung front axle with four-link location at both ends and small-block Chevy power. Bonnet is an original English item with the louvres on a raised panel*

ABOVE *If one's good, two must be better. Unless it's just a reflection of a beautifully detailed Ford V8. Note the old drag racing style weed-spreader headers*

RIGHT *Need we say more? Other than to tell you that obviously George and Linda Lynch of the Okolona Street Rods club have a sense of humour. Lavender Phaeton utilizes a Wescott's fibreglass body, Mustang front suspension, Corvette rear suspension and a 252 cu. in. Buick V6 engine*

CAUTION
THIS ROD HAS HERPES
DON'T TOUCH!

ABOVE *This pick-up probably hauls ass*

After the war California was packed full of young men returned from battle and looking for some of the lost excitement. They found it for the most part in hotted-up cars. Detroit had been working for the war effort, there had been no new models since 1940 and besides it was more interesting to build your own car which invariably would be faster than anything Detroit produced.

The lakes scene grew in popularity and sometimes there would be as many as 500 cars out there. Unfortunately this intense activity was destroying the very surface the racers demanded. New venues had to be found and at this point the hot rod story took two distinct directions.

One group of rodders went up to Utah to establish a track still used annually on the Bonneville salt flats. The other group began to develop what was little more than a traffic light

15

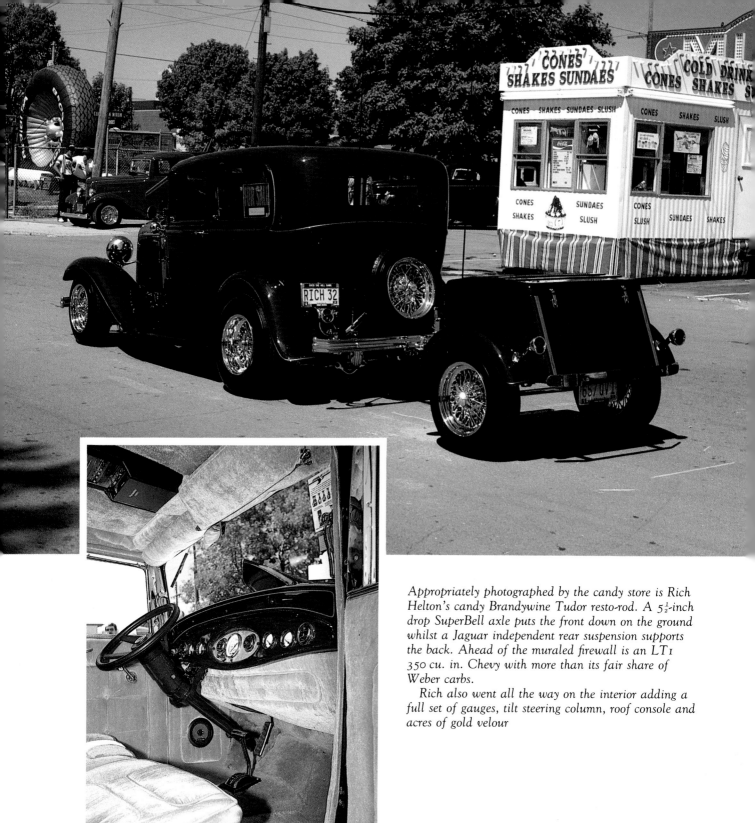

Appropriately photographed by the candy store is Rich Helton's candy Brandywine Tudor resto-rod. A $5\frac{1}{2}$-inch drop SuperBell axle puts the front down on the ground whilst a Jaguar independent rear suspension supports the back. Ahead of the muraled firewall is an LT1 350 cu. in. Chevy with more than its fair share of Weber carbs.

Rich also went all the way on the interior adding a full set of gauges, tilt steering column, roof console and acres of gold velour

grand prix into a major motor sport which became known as drag racing. In all of this activity the Ford V8, and to a great extent the '32 Ford itself, played a major role.

In the thick of all this activity was Robert E. Petersen, publisher of *Hot Rod* magazine, the bible of this fast-growing movement. Not that he had any trouble doing so, but to fill the pages Bob covered every aspect of this sport, from the lakes to lookalike cars which were only driven on the street. The publication of a monthly magazine, the organization of regular drag races on airfields in and around Los Angeles and car shows caused an even more dramatic growth of interest. Pretty soon the hot rod movement was the fastest growing activity in America and a 1932 Ford, nicknamed 'The Deuce', with a Ford V8, was the car to be seen in.

As roadster fever was spreading throughout California and elsewhere, converts in other parts of the country were finding that stripped-down roadsters with no tops, upholstery or even floorboards in some cases might be fine for the West Coast but they were totally impractical in the colder parts of America. Not only that but only

Southern California had dry lakes and drag strips
to race on. Elsewhere hot rods were driven
exclusively on the street and things like paint,
chrome and upholstery became more important.

Ford cars and engines, the '32 and the flathead in
particular, reigned supreme until the mid-1950s
when Chevrolet came out with its powerful, high-
revving ohv V8. Suddenly the flathead Ford V8 was
obsolete and everybody was busy swapping them
for the small-block Chevys.

The general face of the sport was changing too.
The older-style cars were giving way to specially
built race cars, and as Detroit at last discovered the

ABOVE *You see plenty of American campers with a
dirtbike hung on the back, but something this shiny is a
rare sight. The Phaeton is owned by Ray Newman and
the bike is a pretty rare but extremely restored 1946
Whizzer*

ABOVE RIGHT *This candy three-window is about as
clean as they come*

youth market to factory hot rods. Through the 1960s the '32 Ford was all but forgotten except on the show car circuit where many a Deuce was customized (read 'distorted') almost beyond recognition.

Though probably not recognized at the time a significant event occurred in 1970 when a group of rodders formed the National Street Rod Association and held the first-ever Street Rod Nationals in a farmer's field in Peoria, Illinois. Several hundred cars, many of them '32 Fords, turned up and since then the Nats has grown into one of North America's biggest motoring events

attracting annually almost 7000 participating cars. Many of the photographs in this book were taken at various National events.

Then in 1973 a young, almost unknown film director called George Lucas released an autobiographical movie about one night in California in 1962 called *American Graffiti*. The star was nothing other than a canary yellow Deuce Coupé and as it flashed across the cinema screens of the world it introduced a whole new generation to the pleasures of hot rodding. To begin with people could only copy the Graffiti coupé but as they began to understand what it was all about they

realized that there was more to the Deuce than yellow paint and five windows.

Thus began the renaissance. The sport, hobby, call it what you will, is bigger than ever and getting bigger every day as is the industry which supports it, and the 1932 Ford continues to play a significant part as the definitive rod. Any style is acceptable from the nostalgic look of the 1950s to the hi-tech aluminium look of the 1980s. It doesn't seem to matter how you build them as long as you build them. And this book is a tribute to those who have made the effort—hopefully they had a lot of fun on the way and hopefully they are enjoying the fruits of their labours. It is also a tribute to Henry Ford and his team who gave us the toy which has provided so much pleasure.

RIGHT *Except for the candy flames, dropped headlight bar, flying quail and gleaming chrome this five-window coupé belonging to Jim and Chris Haig could be almost original. The small-block Chevy gives it away though*

ABOVE *It might be tight but it fits. It is a 454 cu. in.*
Chevy and it's in a Roadster

ABOVE *There's always room for a pretty girl, even in a two-seater hi-boy. This one mixes traditional style with smooth bonnet sides and up-to-date, independent front suspension with coil-over shocks*

When the family grows up most Roadster owners opt for something with more space. Not this guy. He's built a weather-proof shelter around the rumble seat. Roadster runs Ardun flathead with four twin-choke Webers

ABOVE *Built by Li'l John Buttera this chopped three-window was the first of the hi-tech Deuces. It featured Deuce Factory rails, Buttera-built independent suspension with Koni coil-overs, Fiat rack and pinion steering, Halibrand quick-change differential, a 340 cu. in. Mopar engine with Weslake cylinder heads, Weber carbs and one of the slickest bodies anybody had ever seen. So radical was this car it inspired hundreds of hot rodders to attempt a new approach to age-old problems*

ABOVE *When you're hot, you're hot. And this flamed Tudor belonging to Robb Beard of Hyattsville, Maryland, is definitely one of the hottest. This dangerous Deuce sports a 351 cu. in. Windsor Ford with factory Webers, Crane cam and Vertex magneto.*

    A 4½-inch chop and dropped SuperBell axle get things down on the ground whilst a Corvette column and Mustang steering do the turning, and Mustang and Strange discs do the stopping. Incidentally the licence plate reads, DAMAGE

ABOVE AND RIGHT '32 SKIDOO, *a chopped and beautifully pin-striped Tudor, was running a FR SALE licence plate. It worked too*

ABOVE *It ain't easy being green unless, of course, you want to be photographed at night*

ABOVE *A three-window caught cruising on the Ohi-way*

ABOVE *Is he making a turn signal or just hanging his arm out in the breeze?*

OVERLEAF *Smooth-sided, whited-out, bob-tailed Roadster*

ABOVE *You'd be right in thinking that that plate might indicate a woman owner. Her name is Karen Cotton and she comes from Minnesota. Her top-chopped Tudor is powered by a 305 cu. in. Chevy hooked to a Turbo 400 gearbox and it sports a tilt column, cruise control, power brakes and tinted glass. It was built for her by husband Bruce.*

RIGHT *If you look carefully you can see that Bob Hill's Cabriolet runs independent front suspension and coil-over shocks*

PREVIOUS PAGE *Hi-boys look good whichever way you build them and whichever body style you choose*

ABOVE *Steve Hardin of Chesterfield, Indiana,
specializes in producing machined aluminium parts for
other rodders. However, his own hi-boy Roadster is
rather traditional with its buggy-sprung front end,
Corvette rear and old-timey wire wheels. Nevertheless,
there is a superb milled aluminium dash, sadly out of
sight*

ABOVE Street Rodder *magazine publisher Tom McMullen built this hi-boy tub as a project car. It has the best of everything: 350 cu. in. Chevy with 6-71 blower, Doug Nash five-speed transmission, nine-inch Ford rear axle, dropped I-beam front axle with Mustang disc brakes, Chevy Vega steering, Vintage Hal wheels and a completely chromed undercarriage. Nevertheless, there are some rather odd features including the slotted aluminium grille insert and the down-facing side-panel louvres.*

Rod Broadway's Roadster combines traditional styling and hi-tech appointments, the latter including milled aluminium windscreen posts, Center Line Champ 500 wheels and a three-piece hood under which resides a small-block Chevy with four twin-choke Webers

Black is beautiful, especially in the case of 'Roarin' 30s'
club member Jim Rench's three-window coupé.
Particularly unusual is the rear-hinged three-piece hood
which is integral with the top part of the grille shell.
The grille is equally interesting in that it is formed from
aluminium and has horizontal instead of vertical bars.
Other unusual details include the spreader bar-mounted
turn indicators, spoon-shaped headlight mounts and
beam axle with coil-over suspension

RIGHT *Even with the wind in your hair and the bugs in your teeth, riding in the rumble is the coolest way to enjoy a hot day in Ohio*

BELOW *Victoria's bustle decorated with rather unusual graphics is nevertheless attractive*

44

Black sedan with three-inch top chop and neat pin-stripes sports one of the biggest engines available—an L88 454 cu. in. big-block Chevy fitted with triple carbs

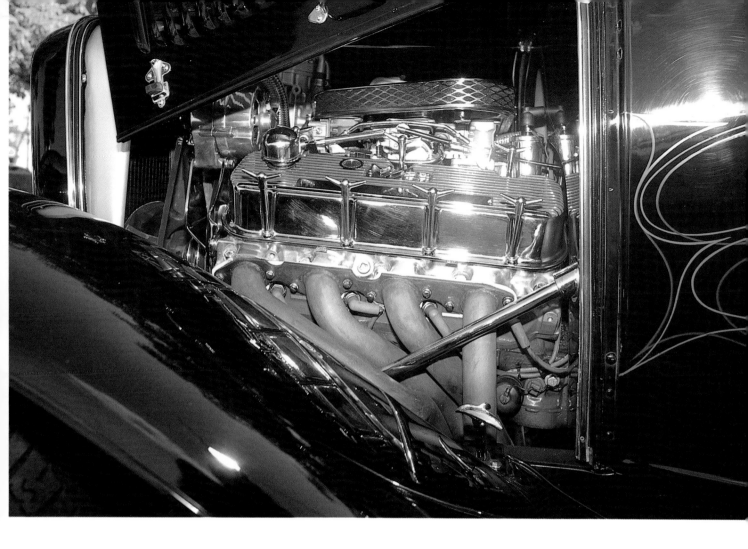

Travelling back in time is Mark Van Acker from
Sussex, New Jersey. Five-inch top-chopped pick-up rides
on a dropped I-beam front axle with '40 Ford brakes
and a '56 Olds rear end. We guess there's enough
power produced by that 1957 Chrysler hemi engine to
boil those skinny whitewall tyres

49

ABOVE *Unusual Sedan Delivery has a channelled body, suicide front end and big-block Ford power*

ABOVE *Getting through the crowd at the Street Rod*
Nationals is not always easy as the owner of this
Victoria is finding out

OVERLEAF *Simply red*

ABOVE *It looks like the owner of this pick-up is having a little half shaft trouble*

ABOVE *Problems at the rear end seem to be common as the owner of this five-window had to get out and get under*

Sadly Swede Tommy Lindblom's Roadster caught fire
not long after these photographs were taken. Before the
tragedy it sported an LT1 350 cu. in. Chevy bored to
362 cu. in. and fitted with $11\frac{1}{2}$:1 pistons, solid lifter
cam, and four Weber 48s on a Moon manifold.
Transmission was a four-speed Muncie connected to a
Jaguar independent rear suspension. Up front an
I-beam axle supports Dunlop wire wheels. The rears are
Appliance. Tommy is a member of the Swedish Street
Rod Association

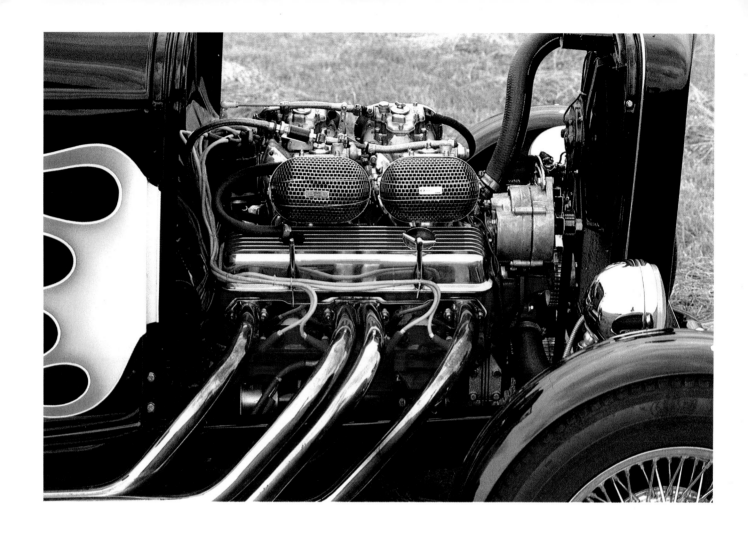

ABOVE, LEFT AND OVERLEAF *Salmon enchanted evening, courtesy of Per-åke Karlsson of Stockholm, Sweden. Fellow Swede Erik Hanson built the repro frame, boxed it and added a drop-out gearbox mount plus a Model A front crossmember to support the transverse leaf spring and SuperBell I-beam axle fitted with Volvo disc brakes. Out back there's an eight-inch Ford rear end. The nicely detailed Radar wheels are shod with a combination of Goodyear and BF Goodrich tyres and turned by means of Chevy Vega cross-steering. Power is provided by a 327 cu. in. Chevy engine with Holley induction hooked to a Turbo 350 gearbox. Incidentally the fibreglass body is also a Swedish product, this time from Speciality Fiberglass*

Christer Carlbaum, a member of the 'Easy Rodders' club, is from Bromma in Sweden. His Victoria rides on a TCI repro chassis with a 4½-inch drop SuperBell front axle and nine-inch Ford rear. The rear drums and front discs are Mustang, as is the steering. The wheels, shod with BF Goodrich tyres, are McLean wires. Power is provided by a 327 cu. in. Chevy rated at 375 bhp. Engine modifications include fitment of an HR 179 cam, high-compression pistons, Mickey Thompson

heads, Offenhauser manifold, 650 Holley carb and
Corvette ignition. Incidentally, this Vicky is fitted with
a two-speed wiper, something Christer says you must
have in Sweden. Does this mean they have two-speed
rain?

ABOVE, LEFT AND OVERLEAF *HOT TUB is an appropriate name for S. Foster Yancey, jun.'s Phaeton. This Dallas, Texas, car may not be the biggest but it certainly has the best. Starting with the frame this is a specially built tubular assembly constructed by Jim Petrykowski. It is suspended on a Posie spring, four-inch drop tube axle mounted with Mustang disc brakes and located by polished stainless steel four-bar links. The rear end is a nine-inch Ford fitted with a Detroit Locker posi and converted to disc brakes. It's located by three polished stainless links and suspended on coil-over shocks. Controlling the Zenith wire wheels and Michelin radials is a Vega cross-steering assembly.*

Motivation is provided by the ubiquitous 350 cu. in. Chevy, uprated in this case with a Competition Cams cam, Z-28 heads, Edelbrock manifold, Carter carb and polished stainless steel tubular headers.

Externally the car is equally modified in that the Porsche Guards Red fibreglass body had the door handles removed and has been fitted with hidden door hinges, aluminium windshield posts, special tail-lights, a sunken licence plate and a three-piece hood.

The hi-tech interior incorporates acres of Wilton carpet, Connolly leather and brushed aluminium.

Not satisfied with this masterpiece, Yancey, jun., is also working on a Victoria and a Roadster

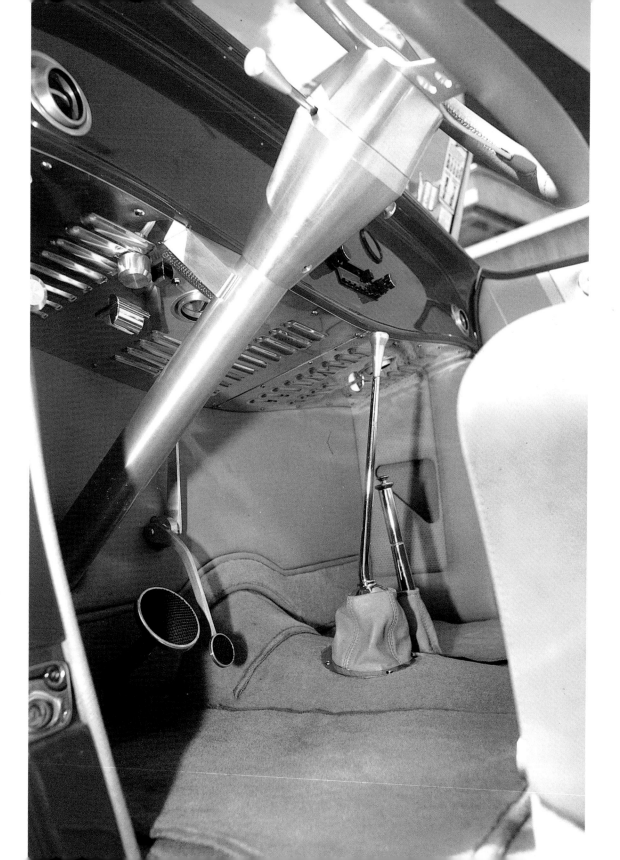

ABOVE AND PAGES 69–75 *There are not many cars one could genuinely call Super but underneath the 120 coats of Adams Red, Randy Ramey's coupé is one exception. The chassis and body began life on Henry's production line but almost everything else is custom built. The three-window body was chopped $4\frac{1}{2}$ inches in front and $3\frac{1}{2}$ inches at the back, to give it a slight rake, then mounted on a chassis equipped with a Super Rod Shop independent front end and a narrowed nine-inch Ford rear. Ford rack and pinion steering is used to guide the custom-built billet aluminium wheels shod with Goodyear NCT tyres.*

Under the louvred three-piece hood resides an
aluminium adorned 331 cu. in. Chevy V8 induced by
triple Rochester 32s with Nitrous Oxide and water
injection.

The interior of 'Super Coupé' is perhaps its most
radical feature with almost everything, except the
Recaro seats and Zora Arkus Duntov steering wheel,
being milled from aluminium by Bob Reid before being
anodized red.

The regular, if you can call it that, upholstery work
was executed by the Pompano Trim Shop

Joliet Jim Talaga of Illinois can be justly proud of this cover car as he performed almost all of the work on it himself. Beginning with the chassis he boxed the rails before adding the traditional dropped front axle and nine-bolt Ford rear. However, here's where tradition stopped, for Jim mounted the rear axle on Chevy Corvair coil springs and damped the whole car with MG lever-arm shocks. Unusual, but Jim assures everybody it works fine.

No Chevy V8 for this guy either—instead he chose a 302 cu. in. Ford, chromed everything he could unbolt, built his own inlet manifold and stainless steel exhaust system and mated it all to a C4 transmission. The rare

Cabriolet body received some massaging in the form of a
two-inch chop before being coated with Jim's own
candy-wine paint mix. Then it was off to the trim shop
where Jim Larsen of Larsen's Auto Trim fabricated the
custom top and upholstered the cut-down stock seat.
Steering the Cadillac wires is a '68 Chevelle tilt column
connected to '72 Econoline steering box converted to
cross-steering

ABOVE, RIGHT AND OVERLEAF *One way to stop your wife from using your street rod is to build her one of her own and that's just what Jim Hodges of Old Hickory, Tennessee, did for his wife Judy.*

Starting with a Total Performance chassis Jim added a nine-inch Ford rear end, buggy-sprung front, Mustang steering and 350 cu. in. Chevy power. Center Line Champ 500 wheels shod with BF Goodrich tyres were hung on each corner and the rolling chassis was ready for a body. Jim chose a fibreglass Roadster from Wescott's and then had Shockley's Body Shop massage the cowl area around the windshield and tidy up the wheel wells before applying some GM Woodland Haze paint and graphics by Harris. The interior was upholstered in contrasting leather by Griffey to complement the Grant wheel and milled aluminium dash

LEFT Inside the infamous Barry Lobeck's shop, recently relocated to Cleveland, Ohio. However, we don't think that's an identikit picture of him hanging on the door. Nevertheless, it has all the right parts as does the Roadster coming together in the foreground

ABOVE Another angle inside Lobeck's reveals a rare and beautifully rodded Station Wagon. Built for Don Smith of Bedford, Texas, by Boyd Coddington, it was styled by artist Thom Taylor and features typical smooth hi-tech finish with traditional mechanics. Roy Brizio built the buggy-sprung frame on to which was lowered a restored but chopped woodie body with raked windshield posts

ler, California

LEFT *Jerry Kugel of Kugel Komponents in Whittier, California, builds these exquisite coil-over, independent front suspension assemblies in stainless steel complete on a weld-in crossmember*

ABOVE *This could be the start of something*

LEFT AND PREVIOUS PAGE
It doesn't seem to matter which way you build a Deuce—it always looks good. Fully channelled body is out of vogue right now but you can bet the owner of this tri-carb'd Deuce enjoys the hell out of his hot rod

ABOVE *It's not the angle—this Deuce is slightly
sectioned*

ABOVE *Any Friday night in Anywhere, America*

ABOVE AND OVERLEAF *Nifty 1950s-style Roadster is the property of Mark Congorth of New Jersey*

LEFT *Jerry's Drive-Inn is the place to be on a Friday night in Columbus, Ohio, especially if you have a hot-rodded Deuce*

ABOVE *I wonder if the spreader bar slogan, 'HE WHO DIES WITH THE MOST TOYS WINS', applies to broken ones*

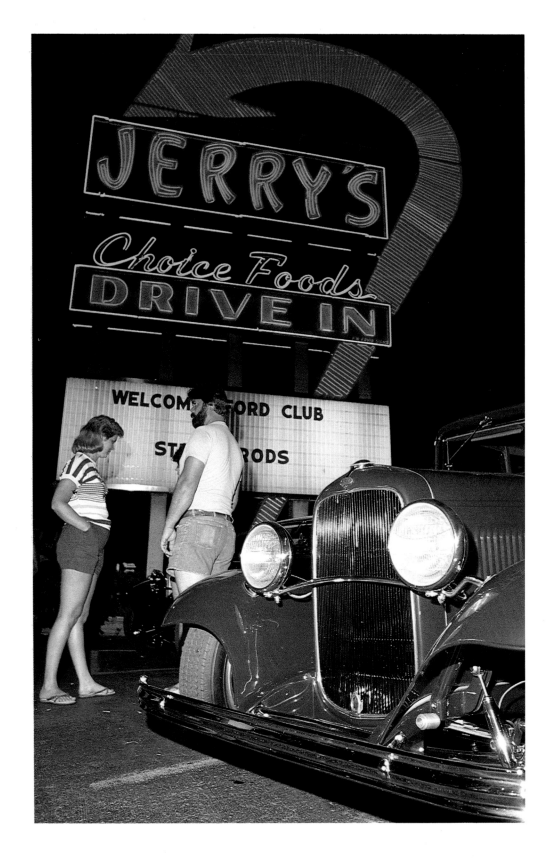

LEFT *At the Drive-Inn*

ABOVE *Pick-up tricks*

ABOVE *When you look at this five-window you can understand how Henry got it almost right. If only he'd chromed the wires, dropped the headlight bar and added yellow to the colour chart*

RIGHT *When it seemed almost impossible to find an original '32 Ford in England a rodder called Geoff Jago decided to manufacture his own chassis and fibreglass body to suit. This Roadster version built by Phil Rutherford is without a doubt the best example. It is powered by an all-aluminium Rover V8 engine induced by a 390 Holley carb on an Offenhauser manifold. Transmission consists of a Borg-Warner 35 gearbox and a Jaguar independent rear suspension, and this chrome and candy show rolls on Tru-Spoke wires*

Besides the guitar the other passion in Jeff Beck's life is street rods, in particular the '32 Ford variety. At the last count he owned eight: two Tudors, two five-window coupés, two three-windows and two Roadsters

ABOVE A semi-restored original three-window which has since received a new chassis from Roy Brizio, a small-block Chevy engine and a black paintjob

RIGHT An American Tudor sedan which has been totally rebuilt since these photographs were taken

OVERLEAF Two of the completed cars are still more or less as pictured, at least the candy-red three-window is. The black five-window could be a blown hi-boy coupé in California by now

RIGHT *Hollywood hi-boy—well, it's Jeff Beck flying on the freeway in his Brizio-rebuilt Roadster. The car is real steel with small-block Chevy power*

OVERLEAF *An old scout hut housed, until recently, two more Deuces. On the left, a Graffiti-lookalike five-window authentic in every detail except for the rare Man-A-Free inlet manifold for which Jeff is still searching. On the right, Super Prune which is now back in America. This one-time show car built by Phil Kendrick needed to be somewhere dry and England just isn't. Consequently the cars are in a more or less constant state of rebuild. With the exception of plating and other impossible-to-do-in-your-backyard jobs, Jeff does all his own work including engine assembly, wiring and quite often painting*

PREVIOUS PAGE *This must be about as low as one can go. Chopped, channelled and sectioned Tudor belongs to short-order chef Kelly Puckett of New Albany, Ohio. Car has since been repainted red and fitted with Center Line Champ 500 wheels. It also features a homemade chassis, full independent suspension and Chevy power*

ABOVE AND PAGES 111–115 *This Roadster belongs to Osprey editor Tony Thacker but was built as a project car during his spell as editor of Custom Car magazine. Built on original but bobbed rails with an English fibreglass body, it incorporates a blend of traditional and modern styling.*

The stainless steel front axle, fitted with a SuperBell hi-boy brake kit, is suspended on a Posie spring and located by a stainless four-link system. In the rear a Mark 2 Jaguar axle fitted with vented discs is suspended on Spax Eliminator coil-over shocks, and located by four stainless links and a Deuce Factory anti-roll bar.

Compomotive split-rim Ferrari-style wheels shod with Pirelli and BF Goodrich tyres are controlled via a Ford Capri column and Vega cross-steering.

Power is provided by a 3-litre Ford V6 tuned by Swaymar Engineering to produce 182 bhp. David Darby photograph courtesy of Custom Car

LEFT AND PAGES 118–120 *Building a 1950s-style car in England is not easy. There's plenty of old Allard Ford flathead equipment to be found but most everything else has to be imported at great expense from the US. Bernie Chodosh's nostalgic ride was based on a coupé built by Bob Zacci and it utilizes original rails, Model A front crossmember, dropped I-beam axle, '40 Ford brakes, split radius rods and a '40 Ford truck axle with a Culver City Halibrand quick-change.*

The 24-stud engine is vintage '42 and is pepped up with a bore to 239 cu. in., Offenhauser heads, twin Stromberg 97s on a Thickstun manifold under a Thickstun air cleaner and magneto ignition. The gearbox is from '39. The fibreglass body is an English product from American Street Rod Parts and the whole car rides on the tallest, skinniest and whitest tyres. Roger Philips photograph courtesy of Custom Car

117

ABOVE AND OVERLEAF *Benke Bjorkman from Stockholm, Sweden, was responsible for this rather clever five-window conversion for a Cabriolet. As you can see, the roof and side window frames are removable, affording either open-topped or closed motoring.*

In place of the original Ford we find a 327 cu. in. Chevy with a 350 cam, Offenhauser inlet manifold and Carter carb. Behind that there's an M21 Muncie four-speed connected to a Jaguar XJ6 independent rear suspension. The front end is also taken from a Jaguar and consists of the torsion bar independent assembly from an E-type, Koni shocks and Peugeot rack and pinion steering. The whole lot rides on Tru-Spoke wire wheels

ABOVE *Hi-tech hi-boy retains beam-axled suspension and early Halibrand wheels but incorporates more modern accoutrements, which include three-piece hood and square headlights*

ABOVE As Henry would have it, well, almost. Greyhound, dropped headlight bar, custom grille insert and wire wheels put this three-window in the slightly unusual class

OVERLEAF On the left, early-Ford parts supplier C.W. Moss and his rare (they only made 926 worldwide) Convertible Sedan (model number B400). On the right, Pete Eastwood, a Los Angeles-based hot rod builder specializing in '32 Fords, with his primered but signwritten Tudor

Other interesting titles from Osprey

'32 Ford – The Deuce
A formal and sporting history of Ford's first V8 and the Model B
Tony Thacker
192 pages hardback, 200 b/w photographs, 0 85045 594 4

Ford Popular and the Small Sidevalves
The development story of Ford's £100 car – the lowest priced car in the world
Dave Turner
196 pages hardback, 175 b/w photographs, 0 85045 599 6

Ghia – Ford's Carrozzeria
A sensational look at the work of Ford's Italian design studio
David Burgess-Wise
192 pages hardback, 220 b/w photographs, 0 85045 625 8

Tri-Chevy
A colour pictorial celebrating those classic Chevys of 1955—'56 and '57
Mike Key
120 pages, 123 colour photographs, 0 85045 615 0

Lead Sleds
A colourful look at chopped and lowered customs—1935 through 1954
Mike Key
128 pages, 124 colour photographs, 0 85045 547 2

Street Machines
A full colour review of post-'49 street machines and customs
Andrew Morland
128 pages, 122 colour photographs, 0 85045 546 4

Available from all good bookshops or write for a catalogue to: Osprey Publishing, 27A Floral Street, London WC2E 9DP, England.
Motorbooks International, PO Box 2, 729 Prospect Avenue, Osceola, Wisconsin 54020, USA